Jiu-Jitsu

BY DIANA MURRELL

Apex is distributed by North Star Editions:
sales@northstareditions.com | 888-417-0195

Produced for Apex by Red Line Editorial.

Photographs ©: Operation 2022/Alamy, cover; Shutterstock Images, 1, 10–11, 13, 18–19, 21, 22–23, 26, 27; iStockphoto, 4–5, 6–7, 8–9, 16–17, 20, 24, 25, 29; Colin Waters/Alamy, 12; Wikimedia Commons, 14; Feline Lim/Singapore Press/AP Images, 15

Library of Congress Control Number: 2023910169

ISBN
978-1-63738-763-4 (hardcover)
978-1-63738-806-8 (paperback)
978-1-63738-888-4 (ebook pdf)
978-1-63738-849-5 (hosted ebook)

Printed in the United States of America
Mankato, MN
012024

NOTE TO PARENTS AND EDUCATORS

Apex books are designed to build literacy skills in striving readers. Exciting, high-interest content attracts and holds readers' attention. The text is carefully leveled to allow students to achieve success quickly. Additional features, such as bolded glossary words for difficult terms, help build comprehension.

TABLE OF CONTENTS

CHAPTER 1

AT A MATCH

A boy faces his friend in a jiu-jitsu match. The boy throws the first punch. But the friend ducks and strikes back.

In a jiu-jitsu match, fighters begin by standing. They use strikes and grabs to knock each other over.

The friend grabs the boy's wrist. He twists the boy's arm into a wristlock. Then he throws the boy to the mat.

FAST FACT

In jiu-jitsu, some strikes use fists. Others use open hands.

Many jiu-jitsu moves involve throws and falls. So, matches take place on padded mats.

The friend tries to hold the boy down. But the boy rolls over and pins the friend instead. The friend **submits**, and the boy wins the match.

THE GI

Many jiu-jitsu fighters wear a uniform called a gi. A gi has a jacket and pants. A belt holds the jacket closed. The belt's color shows the fighter's skill level.

Fighters submit when they cannot safely get out of a grip or hold.

CHAPTER 2

HiSTORY

Jiu-jitsu was created hundreds of years ago. Japanese **samurai** developed it. They used hits, holds, and throws to attack **opponents**.

Samurai fought many battles in Japan. They were known for their swords and armor.

Yukio Tani was born in 1881. He was one of the first people to teach jiu-jitsu and judo outside Japan.

At first, jiu-jitsu was used in battle. But teachers made less-violent versions, too. By the 1800s, many styles had developed. One became known as judo.

FAST FACT

Jiu-jitsu **inspired** several other martial arts styles. One is aikido. It focuses on **self-defense**.

Aikido teaches ways to stop or avoid opponents' attacks.

In the early 1900s, a judo teacher went to Brazil. He taught Carlos Gracie. Gracie's family started a new martial art style. It was Brazilian jiu-jitsu. This style spread around the world.

Mitsuyo Maeda was a famous fighter from Japan. He taught the Gracie family.

Much of the fighting in Brazilian jiu-jitsu takes place on the ground.

A SIMPLER STYLE

Brazilian jiu-jitsu has fewer moves. Fighters don't use strikes. Instead, they focus on **grappling**. This makes the style easy to learn. It is also safer.

CHAPTER 3

LEARNING Jiu-Jitsu

Jiu-jitsu focuses on using an opponent's force against them. Some moves let fighters **redirect** force. Others target the opponent's weak spots.

Fighters may grab an opponent's gi to help push or pull the person.

Fighters often use their legs to hold or trap parts of an opponent's body.

Fighters learn several kinds of throws and holds. They often grapple on the ground. Fighters use mounts to pin opponents. They sit on opponents and hold them down.

FAST FACT

In choke holds, fighters wrap their arms or legs around an opponent's neck.

Teachers watch students do moves. They give help and decide when students are ready to get new belts.

To learn jiu-jitsu, people often take classes at a school called a dojo. They earn colored belts as they learn more moves.

BELTS

Students start with white belts. Each higher **rank** has a new color. Black belts are at the top. In Brazilian jiu-jitsu, belts can also have stripes. Adding stripes shows skill.

In Brazilian jiu-jitsu, fighters earn four stripes on each belt. Then they get a new belt color.

CHAPTER 4

COMPETING

Japanese jiu-jitsu competitions are rare. But many people compete in Brazilian jiu-jitsu. Fighters are often grouped by weight, age, and rank. They face off in pairs.

Fighters face opponents who are a similar weight. That helps keep matches fair.

Choke holds are a common way to get opponents to submit.

Fighters win matches by getting opponents to submit. They can also earn points. They score points by doing certain moves, such as **takedowns** or mounts.

FAST FACT

If no one submits, the fighter with the most points wins.

Fighters must hold some moves for three seconds to score points.

Events often include several matches. Winners may go on to bigger competitions. Top fighters travel to events around the world. Thousands of people watch.

Top fighters can win medals and prizes.

No-gi fights use different rules and moves.

NO-GI MATCHES

At some events, fighters do not wear gis. Instead, they wear tight-fitting shirts and shorts. Opponents can't grab these clothes. So, no-gi events involve more wrestling-style moves.

COMPREHENSION QUESTIONS

Write your answers on a separate piece of paper.

1. Write a sentence that explains the main idea of Chapter 2.

2. Would you rather study Japanese jiu-jitsu or Brazilian jiu-jitsu? Why?

3. What is a gi?

    A. a school where people study jiu-jitsu

    B. a move that knocks down an opponent

    C. a uniform that jiu-jitsu fighters wear

4. Why would not using strikes make Brazilian jiu-jitsu safer?

    A. Those moves are the hardest to learn.

    B. Those moves are most likely to hurt fighters.

    C. Those moves are least likely to win matches.

5. What does **developed** mean in this book?

Jiu-jitsu was created hundreds of years ago. Japanese samurai developed it.

    A. made something up
    B. stopped doing something
    C. lost something

6. What does **rare** mean in this book?

Japanese jiu-jitsu competitions are rare. But many people compete in Brazilian jiu-jitsu.

    A. done by many people
    B. happening very often
    C. not very common

Answer key on page 32.

GLOSSARY

grappling
Grabbing or holding someone as part of a fight.

inspired
Started or gave the idea for something.

opponents
People that someone is fighting against.

rank
A level of skill or ability.

redirect
To change where something ends up or how it moves.

samurai
Warriors who fought in Japan from the late 1100s to the 1800s.

self-defense
Ways to fight back or stay safe if attacked.

submits
Gives up and ends a fight.

takedowns
Moves that make an opponent fall to the ground.

BOOKS

Brainard, Jason. *Brazilian Jujitsu.* New York: PowerKids Press, 2020.

Corso, Phil. *Jujitsu.* New York: PowerKids Press, 2020.

Krohn, Frazer Andrew. *MMA: Ferocious Fighting Styles.* Minneapolis: Abdo Publishing, 2023.

ONLINE RESOURCES

Visit **www.apexeditions.com** to find links and resources related to this title.

ABOUT THE AUTHOR

Diana Murrell is a writer and teacher. She lives in Canada with her family. Diana likes exploring nature trails when she is not writing.

INDEX

ANSWER KEY:
1. Answers will vary; 2. Answers will vary; 3. C; 4. B; 5. A; 6. C